Tornadoes

By Helen Lepp Friesen

www.av2books.com

AV² provides enriched content that supplements and complements this book. Weigl's AV² books strive to create inspired learning and engage young minds in a total learning experience.

Your AV² Media Enhanced books come alive with...

Audio
Listen to sections of the book read aloud.

Key Words
Study vocabulary, and complete a matching word activity.

Go to **www.av2books.com**, and enter this book's unique code.

Video
Watch informative video clips.

Quizzes
Test your knowledge.

BOOK CODE

N978506

Embedded Weblinks
Gain additional information for research.

Slide Show
View images and captions, and prepare a presentation.

AV² by Weigl brings you media enhanced books that support active learning.

Try This!
Complete activities and hands-on experiments.

... and much, much more!

Published by AV² by Weigl
350 5th Avenue, 59th Floor
New York, NY 10118
Websites: www.av2books.com   www.weigl.com

Library of Congress Control Number: 2014934887

ISBN 978-1-4896-1214-4 (hardcover)
ISBN 978-1-4896-1215-1 (softcover)
ISBN 978-1-4896-1216-8 (single user eBook)
ISBN 978-1-4896-1217-5 (multi-user eBook)

Printed in the United States of America in North Mankato, Minnesota
1 2 3 4 5 6 7 8 9 0 18 17 16 15 14

062014
WEP090514

Senior Editor: Aaron Carr
Art Director: Terry Paulhus

Every reasonable effort has been made to trace ownership and to obtain permission to reprint copyright material. The publishers would be pleased to have any errors or omissions brought to their attention so that they may be corrected in subsequent printings.

Photo Credits
Weigl acknowledges Getty Images as its primary photo supplier for this title.

Can the Earth Survive?

Challenges to Our Energy Supply

Ewan McLeish

New York

Published in 2010 by The Rosen Publishing Group Inc.
29 East 21st Street, New York, NY 10010

First Edition

Commissiong Editor: Jennifer Sanderson
Consultant: Steph Warren (BA, PGCE, GCSE Principal Examiner)
Designer: Jane Hawkins
Picture researcher: Kathy Lockley
Illustrator: Ian Thompson
Proofreader: Susie Brooks

Library of Congress Cataloging-in-Publication Data

McLeish, Ewan, 1950-
    Challenges to our energy supply / Ewan McLeish.
        p. cm.
    Includes bibliographical references and index.
    ISBN 978-1-4358-5357-7 (library binding)
    ISBN 978-1-4358-5490-1 (paperback)
    ISBN 978-1-4358-5491-8 (6-pack)
    1.   Power resources—Juvenile literature. 2.   Energy conservation—
Juvenile literature.   I. Title.
TJ163.2.M385 2010
333.79—dc22

                                                    2008052470

Picture Acknowledgements:
The author and publisher would like to thank the following agencies for allowing these
pictures to be reproduced: Tony Binns/EASI-images: 27; Rob Bowden/EASI-images: 22, 34;
Adrian Cooper/EASI-images: 43 ;Digital Vision/Getty: Cover, 1, 9, 12; Copyright DONG Energy
A/S: 31; Du Huaju/Xinhua Press/Corbis: 45; Brad Loper/Dallas Morning News/Corbis: 7;
Lawrence Manning/Corbis: 15; Marine Current Turbines TM Ltd: 37; Kay Nietfeld/epa/Corbis:
20; Mark Partridge/Rex Features: 5; Clive Sanders/EASI-images: 18; Frederic Soltan/Sangha
Productions/Corbis: 25; David Turnley/Corbis: 11; U.S. DOE Photo: 29, 32, 33, 38, 41

Manufactured in China

Contents

Energy for Everyone

Energy is the capacity to make things happen—to do work. People use energy in almost every aspect of their lives. Energy sources are used to light and heat buildings, power vehicles, cook meals, work machinery, and much more. Without energy, nothing can be done.

Energy All Around

Earth provides sources of energy in many natural forms. These include fossil fuels (coal, oil, and gas), which release energy when they are burned, as well as power from the Sun (solar power), wind, and flowing water (hydropower). Tidal, nuclear (generated by a nuclear reactor), and geothermal power (from heat in rocks) are yet more sources of energy available for people to use.

In many ways, there is no shortage of energy on Earth. Around the world, people consume less than one-hundredth of the Sun's energy reaching the Earth alone. However, the problem is how much of the Earth's energy can be captured in a usable form. Can enough energy to meet considerable human demands be recovered without damaging the planet in the process?

Supply and Demand

The world's population is growing rapidly. Many countries are becoming more industrialized and are using increasing amounts of energy-guzzling technology and machinery. People are consuming nearly twice as much energy as they were 30 years ago. Reserves of fossil fuels, particularly oil and gas, are running low. In addition, conflicts around the world can restrict people's access to energy supplies, even where natural reserves are plentiful.

IT'S A FACT

Almost half of the solar radiation falling on the Earth is absorbed or reflected by the atmosphere. The rest reaches the Earth's surface. If this could be captured, an area the size of a kitchen table could provide enough energy to boil a pan of water!

▲ These truck drivers in England are protesting about the high price of fuel, which threatens their livelihoods. The drivers want their government to reduce the tax on fuel to lessen the effect of rising oil prices.

Running on Empty

You may have experienced a local power cut or fuel dispute before. Perhaps for a few hours, even a day, your lights did not work, you could not watch television, there was no hot water, and the house felt cold. Perhaps there were long lines at a nearby gas station, with people panicking that the pumps would run dry. In many countries, scenarios like this can be common. Iraq, for example, has huge oil reserves, but recent conflict has meant that ordinary people have faced great hardship as oil supplies have been rationed and electricity made available for only limited periods of time. In these situations, hospitals are disrupted, public transportation grinds to a halt, and industry is badly affected. A threat to its energy supplies can throw any country, anywhere in the world, into crisis.

Could the energy crisis become universal in the future, and if so how far into the future might this be? Could a point be reached where power cuts and fuel rationing become commonplace in more countries around the world? Will people's use of energy eventually outstrip the world's ability to supply it?

Looking at the Facts

Understanding the extent of the world's energy problems involves answering a number of questions. Where does most of the energy people consume come from, and how is it generally used? How much is left of the world's traditional energy supplies, particularly fossil fuels, and what other sources of energy are available both now and in the future? What is the demand for energy likely to be in years to come; in other words, how much will current populations, and future generations, need?

An Added Problem

A possible future energy shortage is not the only aspect of the energy crisis. Most people now accept that fossil fuel use is causing a warming of the Earth. When coal, oil, and natural gas are burned, they produce carbon dioxide and other so-called greenhouse gases. In simple terms, increasing levels of these gases mean that more heat is trapped by the Earth's atmosphere, rather than escaping into space. There are many possible consequences of this (see page 18). All of them, however, are likely to have a major, perhaps catastrophic, impact on human populations around the world.

▼ As carbon dioxide levels in the atmosphere increase, less heat energy can escape; the effect is similar to that in a greenhouse, where light energy is allowed in, then converted into heat, which cannot escape as easily back through the glass.

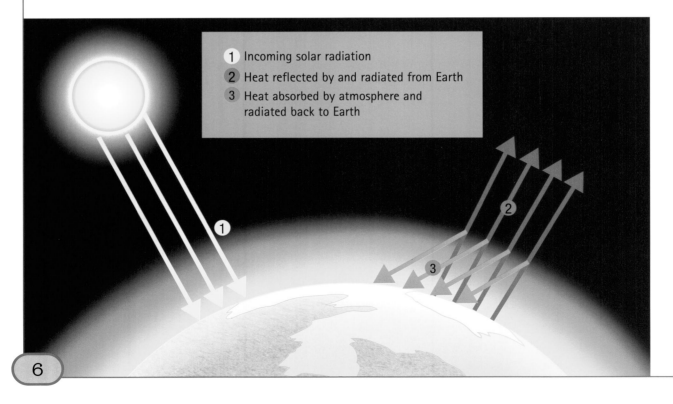

1 Incoming solar radiation
2 Heat reflected by and radiated from Earth
3 Heat absorbed by atmosphere and radiated back to Earth

▲ Sights such as this in New Orleans are likely to become more common as global warming leads to more extreme weather patterns.

Considering the future

Even if people start to rely less on fossil fuels, there is much debate as to how the world's future energy needs will be met. For example, should countries invest in a new generation of nuclear power stations as a way of combating global warming and replacing fossil fuels as they decline? Or should nuclear power be abandoned in favor of more sustainable (and many would argue, safer) technologies? Should scientists explore new methods of energy generation, such as nuclear fusion, which are as yet unproven? And would these give us enough energy in the future, or could the world face an "energy gap" in 20 or 30 years' time, with no realistic way of filling it?

Interdependency

Everything people do is interconnected and has consequences, both for the planet and for other people. This is especially true of the use of energy. Few countries are self-sufficient in energy resources, and the consequences of global warming affect everyone. The message is therefore simple: people have to learn to cooperate more in solving the world's energy needs.

IT'S A FACT

Nuclear fusion copies the nuclear reactions that go on in the Sun. Atoms of hydrogen are combined at temperatures of 180 million degrees Fahrenheit (100 million degrees Celsius) to form helium, releasing energy. In 2006, an experimental reactor built in France cost $7 billion. Because of the cost, many people believe that nuclear fusion will never be a realistic energy source.

The Lowdown on Energy

The type and the source of energy that people use varies around the world, and so does the way people use energy. In some places, much less energy is consumed than in others. However, no person can survive without access to an energy supply of some kind.

Versatile Energy

Energy can take many different forms—thermal (heat), chemical, kinetic (movement), and so on. Some of these forms can be used directly—for example, cooking on an open flame. It is also possible to convert one form of energy to another. For example, kinetic energy can be converted into electrical energy by means of a generator. When this occurs, two things happen: an energy transfer takes place and some energy is "lost" or wasted, usually as heat. This idea is important when it comes to improving energy efficiency. For example, heating a building using fuel, such as gas, directly, is less wasteful than using gas to heat water to produce steam to drive a turbine to create electricity to heat the building, because there are fewer energy conversions.

Energy Everywhere

Most of the energy that is available to people comes from the Sun. This does not mean solar power alone. The Sun also drives the wind and the hydrologic (water) cycle. It once provided life for the plants and animals that over millions of years have decayed to form fossil fuels, and it supplies the energy that enables trees to grow and so supply us with wood. The main exceptions are tidal, nuclear, and geothermal power. Tidal power comes from the gravitational pull of the Moon and the Sun; nuclear energy comes from the forces that hold atoms together; and geothermal energy comes mainly from the radioactive decay of rocks deep inside the Earth.

Renewable or Nonrenewable

The world's energy reserves can be divided into renewable and nonrenewable sources. Fossil fuels are considered nonrenewable resources, because the rate at which they are used far exceeds the rate at which they are being formed. The same is true of the mineral uranium, which is used in nuclear power stations. On the other hand, renewable resources, such as the Sun and wind, do not decrease with use. They still come at a cost, however. Whatever energy sources the world chooses in the future, people will have to balance the benefits against the economic and environmental price they will have to pay. For example, the United Kingdom. is promoting the expansion of nuclear power because it contributes relatively little to global warming. Nuclear power is expensive, however, and many people still oppose it on safety and environmental grounds (see page 20).

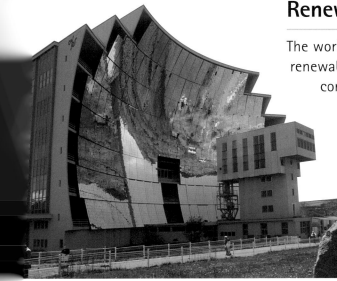

▲ This solar collector in the French Pyrenees has 63 parabolic mirrors that track the Sun and focus its rays onto a 10-ton boiler. It is capable of generating 1 megawatt (MW) of power.

Evidence

USING RESOURCES

This pie chart shows that over 85 percent of the energy used worldwide still comes from fossil fuels. The figures in this chart are for what is called commercial energy. This is energy that is bought or sold. It does not include the fuelwood that is collected around the world; this makes up about 4 percent of all the energy consumed (see page 22).

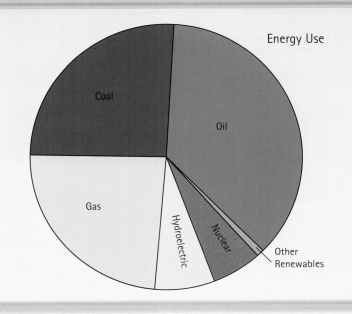

Use of Energy

In more economically developed countries (MEDCs), much of the energy consumed is in the form of electricity, because this is a convenient way to run machines and appliances. Fuels such as oil, gas, and coal, however, are also burned directly to provide heat energy for industry or homes. In many parts of the world, particularly in less economically developed countries (LEDCs), wood is often burned as the main energy source. How people use energy affects their attitude toward it. Many people are used to having almost unlimited energy supplies literally at their fingertips. They seldom think about how much they use, or the impact that use may be having. And few people ever give much thought to what would happen if the Earth's energy really did start to run out.

▶ This family in rural South Africa spends much of its time gathered around this wood-burning stove. The fumes from the fire are potentially harmful, and the use of fuelwood may be damaging the surrounding woodland.

CASE STUDY
Two Lives Compared

Ruud lives in a large house in Amsterdam in the Netherlands. His home is heated in the winter and air-conditioned in the summer. He is never short of hot water, good lighting, or cooked meals. He usually takes the bus to school, but sometimes one of his parents drives him in one of the family's two cars. His school is also heated and well lit. Ruud enjoys the benefits of many different manufactured goods and goes on vacation twice a year. To supply this, he uses an average of 150 kWh of energy each day. This is enough energy to boil three large pans of water continuously.

Daljeet is less fortunate than Ruud. Her home is a small, corrugated-iron shack in a shanty town outside Nairobi in Kenya. There is no heating in her house and sometimes the nights are very cold. Daljeet uses light from candles (or a hurricane lamp, if her family can afford the kerosene fuel) to finish her homework. She helps to cook the family meal using an inefficient wood stove, which produces dangerous fumes that are slowly damaging her health. She has few possessions and she does not take vacations. Daljeet uses an average of 5 kWh of energy per day. This is 30 times less energy than Ruud uses, and it is about enough to bring a large pot of water to the boiling point.

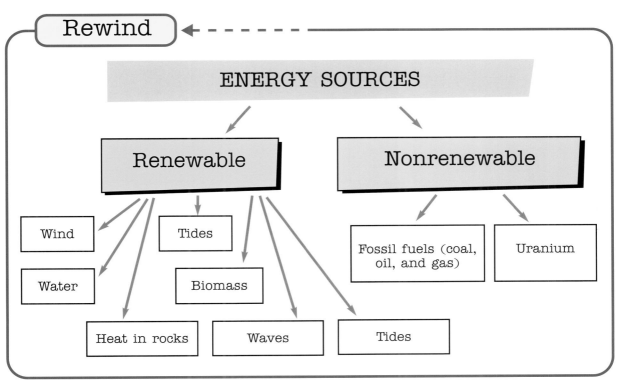

World Energy Status

Looking at the world's energy status reveals a varied picture. Not only do different parts of the world consume different amounts of energy, but they produce different amounts, too. Natural resources vary from region to region—as does the ability to generate power. So who are the world's big energy producers and who are the energy "have-nots"?

▲ This oil rig is in the North Sea. As this source of oil and gas declines, the United Kingdom will need to find other sources of energy.

The Energy Rich

Figures show that the United States is by far the world's biggest producer of energy, followed by the Middle East and China. These enormous regions have extensive natural resources. The United States generates most of its energy from a combination of fossil fuels (mainly oil) and nuclear power, and the Middle East is rich in oil and gas and China has huge deposits of coal. Within Europe, Norway produces more than one-fifth of the continent's energy, most of it coming from hydroelectric power (HEP). Meanwhile, France obtains 80 percent of its electricity from nuclear power. These differences in energy source are important when it comes to looking at the world's future energy supplies.

The Energy Poor

Some countries have very few natural energy resources of their own. They struggle to meet their power needs and are forced to buy energy from abroad. Excluding its top four energy producers—Nigeria, Algeria, Angola, and Libya—Africa produces only 9.32 Qbtu

Evidence

WORLD ENERGY PRODUCTION

This bar chart shows the energy production for regions per year. The U.S.A. is the leading energy producer with just over 70 Qbtu per year. Although Africa is low down the list, it is still a major "energy power" thanks to oil-rich countries such as Algeria and Nigeria.

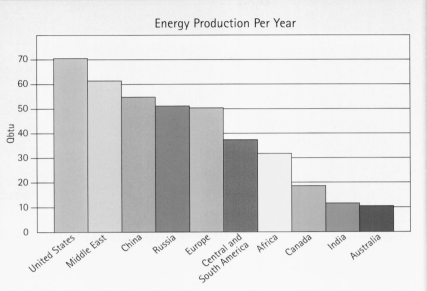

Energy Production Per Year

(Quadrillion British Thermal Units) in total per year less than the output of Norway—and that is between more than 50 countries. One Qbtu is equivalent to 172 million barrels of oil and one U.K. barrel is 50 gallons (190 liters). Energy is an expensive commodity and poor countries find imports difficult to afford. As we have seen, a lack of energy means that industrial development, transportation, basic services, such as schools and hospitals, and domestic needs all suffer.

Tipping the Balance

Not all energy-poor countries are poor themselves. Japan is low in natural energy resources, with a primary energy production of around 4 Qbtu. It therefore relies heavily on imported oil and gas, as well as uranium for its 55 nuclear reactors. Japan is a wealthy country, however, and for the time being, it can afford to buy the energy it needs. Other countries, such as Nigeria, are energy rich but still remain poor. And some poor countries do not have the technology to harness potential energy sources, such as solar power.

IT'S A FACT

Nigeria exports $30 billion worth of oil a year. Although Nigeria gives 13 percent of its oil revenues to help develop its oil-producing regions, much of this is siphoned off by corrupt officials or wasted on projects that do little to help ordinary people.

Where Does it All Go?

Comparing figures for energy production and consumption within a country reveals interesting differences. Some countries or regions are known as net producers of energy—they produce more than they consume themselves. Others are called net consumers—they use more energy than they produce.

Although the United States is the biggest producer, its consumption of energy still outstrips its production by some way—making it a net consumer. The same is true of Europe, Japan, and South Korea. Areas such as the Middle East, Russia, and Central and South America are net producers. Africa, despite being quite low in production, still ranks as a net producer, because it consumes very little commercial energy. This is because most of the continent is much less developed than many other parts of the world.

Evidence

WORLD ENERGY CONSUMPTION

Compare this table with the one on page 13. The United States heads both lists. It is the top producer and the top consumer of energy. Europe is the next-biggest consumer—not far behind the United States, using over 85 Qbtu of energy a year. China and Russia are third and fourth in both groups. The Middle East, second as a producer, comes lower in the table for consumption.

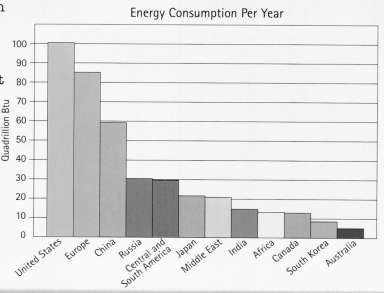

Energy Consumption Per Year

(Quadrillion Btu)

Who Uses the Energy?

It is also important to understand exactly where energy goes within a country or region. This means looking at how energy consumption is divided between the various sectors, such as transportation, industry, and domestic or residential. Again the figures vary between the richer and poorer parts of the world.

The OECD (Organization for Economic Cooperation and Development) represents a group of mainly industrialized countries, covering wealthier regions such as the United States, Europe, Australia, and Japan. The non-OECD regions tend to be poorer but include rapidly developing giants such as China, India, and South America. As you might expect, OECD countries use a greater proportion of energy on transportation and commercial buildings.

Although total energy consumption is greater among the OECD nations overall, non-OECD countries use more energy on industry than the richer nations (90 Qbtu compared to 71 Qbtu for the OECDs). How these non-OECD countries continue to develop will be a vital factor in determining whether or not the world might soon be running out of energy.

▲ As air travel becomes cheaper and more popular, the air industry has become the fastest-growing consumer of energy. Some airlines are considering the use of biomass fuels (see page 32) as a way of reducing their dependence on fossil fuels and combating global warming.

What is Left?

Establishing how much remains of the world's nonrenewable energy sources—fossil fuels and uranium—is not easy. Figures detail "known" reserves, but there may be others that have not yet been discovered. As exploration and extraction techniques become more advanced, new reserves may become available.

Coal

There is no shortage of coal in the ground. Reserves are probably 15 times that of oil or gas, and are found mostly in China and the former U.S.S.R. New technologies make it possible to convert coal into more efficient liquid fuels, and even jet fuel. However, coal is still regarded as a dirty fuel, because of the large amounts of carbon it emits when it is burned.

Oil

If production continues at the present rate, known global oil reserves will last for another 40 years. However, these reserves are concentrated in certain parts of the world, particularly the Middle East. Here, oil could last for another 80 years, but in the United States, for example, estimates suggest reserves will

▼ This map shows the remaining reserves of oil by region in billions of barrels in 2006. The proven reserves increase as improved technology and further exploration opens up new areas.

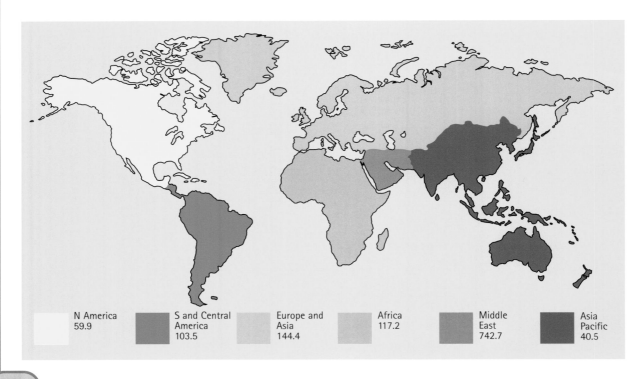

| N America 59.9 | S and Central America 103.5 | Europe and Asia 144.4 | Africa 117.2 | Middle East 742.7 | Asia Pacific 40.5 |

Current drilling technology can drill for oil in up to 1.9 miles (3 kilometers) depth of water—but one-half of the ocean is deeper than this and may have reserves far below.

run low in as little as 12 years. It is generally agreed that the peak of production worldwide will occur in 2020. After this, production will decline as extracting what remains becomes more difficult.

Gas

Reserves of natural gas are lower than for oil, but production and consumption are also lower, meaning that peak production may be reached in 30 years, with reserves exhausted within 70 years. More countries are now turning to gas for electricity generation, because it produces lower carbon emissions than coal or oil. Increased production rates would therefore deplete reserves more rapidly.

Uranium

The International Atomic Energy Authority estimates uranium resources to be almost ten times greater than those of coal. This assumes that the latest "fast breeder" reactors will recycle nuclear fuel, and in effect, produce more fissile material (material capable of undergoing nuclear fission) than they consume. If this is not the case, reserves of uranium are much more limited, perhaps similar to those of oil and gas.

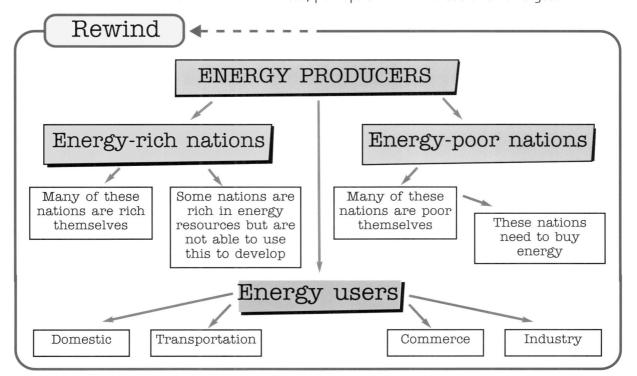

Rewind

ENERGY PRODUCERS

Energy-rich nations

Many of these nations are rich themselves

Some nations are rich in energy resources but are not able to use this to develop

Energy-poor nations

Many of these nations are poor themselves

These nations need to buy energy

Energy users

Domestic

Transportation

Commerce

Industry

The Cost of Doing Nothing

People need to make some changes to the ways in which they produce and consume energy. There are many signs that if these changes do not happen, the Earth may struggle to survive.

Fossil Fuels—A Global Crisis?

There seems to be little doubt that the world's climate is changing. The degree to which this is happening—and the exact consequences—are less certain. Most scientists now agree, however, that global climate change is occurring due to the continued (and increasing) use of carbon-emitting fossil fuels.

▼ A glacier in Antarctica "calves" new icebergs as it reaches the sea. This is a natural process but the speed at which this is occurring is increasing rapidly.

IT'S A FACT

Average temperatures have increased by 1.4° F (0.8° C) since 1880. Arctic ice is disappearing and the region may have its first completely ice-free summer by 2040 or earlier.

ome of the effects of climate change re well known. They include the faster elting of the polar ice caps, rising sea vels, and warming of the Earth's oceans. hey also include changing weather atterns and an increase in extreme weather, such as hurricanes, heavy rains, nd droughts. All of these have further effects on plant, animal, and human populations. Habitat change, coral damage, and the decline of plankton leading to the collapse of marine food chains, have all been recorded. Crop failures, flooding, and devastating damage to whole communities may be the price humans pay.

LEDCs are those most likely to be worst hit. This is partly due to the fact that many of them are in low-lying areas, and partly because they are already subject to more violent weather patterns. The cyclones that hit Myanmar in May 2008, causing widespread flooding of the Irriwadi Delta, killed many tens of thousands of people and made hundreds of thousands homeless and destitute. As well as being more vulnerable to climate change, poor countries are less able to deal with the aftermath of such devastation.

Willing to Share?

Climate change is not the only factor to consider. The distribution of fossil fuels throughout the world is very uneven. Some regions, with limited reserves, already depend on foreign imports for their energy needs. Others may soon do so. This may lead to increased tensions between countries as governments seek to safeguard their energy supplies. Some people believe that the two Gulf Wars in Iraq in 1990–1 and 2003 were partly motivated by this idea.

CASE STUDY
Capturing Carbon

It is technically possible to capture carbon dioxide (CO_2) from major emitters, such as power stations, and then store it permanently, effectively cutting the amount of carbon released into the atmosphere. The technology, known as carbon capture and storage (CCS), may involve capture either after combustion of the fuel, or beforehand. For example, coal can be "gasified" to form hydrogen fuel, with the resulting CO_2 removed.

However, carbon capture is expensive and requires large amounts of energy. In the long run, the carbon could be stored in deep rock formations, deep oceans, or in chemical combination with minerals, but this still is largely untried. CCS plants have already opened in Algeria, Australia, Canada, and Norway, and countries such as the United Kingdom have plans to open plants in the future.

▲ Police guard railroad tracks as nuclear waste is transported in France.

A Nuclear Future?

At the present time, nuclear power provides 15 percent of the world's electricity and 6.5 percent of its energy requirements overall. This could be increased substantially to help fill any future energy gaps, but the world is facing a dilemma. Nuclear power presents a number of issues that have not yet been fully resolved. One is that the safety record of nuclear power stations, although generally good, has suffered some serious setbacks. Perhaps the best known is the disaster in Chernobyl in 1986.

Risky Business

Although the overall damage from Chernobyl was much less than predicted at the time, there have been a number of other accidents, in the U.S.A., the U.K., and Japan, for example. The nuclear power process also creates waste, and the problems associated with the long-term disposal of such waste have not been solved. Also, the possibility of terrorist attacks on nuclear sites cannot be ruled out.

CASE STUDY
Lethal Explosion

In April 1986, a safety drill went wrong at the Chernobyl nuclear plant, Ukraine. The reactor core began to overheat, causing a nonnuclear explosion that tore the top off the concrete containment building housing the reactor. As a result, radioactive material, such as caesium and radioactive iodine, were thrown high into the atmosphere. There it drifted across much of Eastern and northern Europe, contaminating approximately 77,220 square miles (200,000 square km) of land. About 60 people died as a direct result of radiation poisoning, most of them emergency workers dealing with the explosion. Several thousand children who were exposed to the fallout—the airborne radioactive particles—have since contracted thyroid cancer, although most have survived.

Beginning or End?

Many existing nuclear plants are reaching the end of their operational lives and will have to be closed or decommissioned. This is a costly and potentially hazardous operation. Countries with established nuclear power have to decide whether to develop their nuclear programs or to abandon the technology. Some nations, such as Germany and Spain, have decided to phase out their nuclear plants. Others, such as the United States and the United Kingdom, are keeping their options open and have yet to make a final decision. In May 2008, however, the U.K. government gave its strongest indication yet that it intended to replace and then increase its current nuclear capacity. Meanwhile, the United States has submitted a number of applications for new nuclear power stations to be built.

A number of countries are developing nuclear power for the first time, including Iran, North Korea, Australia, Turkey, Indonesia, Vietnam, and Egypt. Some of these countries are in unstable parts of the world where the security of nuclear sites could be a serious issue. Some have even been accused of using their nuclear programs as a "cover" for developing nuclear weapons.

Evidence

NUCLEAR POWER STATIONS

There are currently 435 nuclear power stations in operation worldwide, with a further 30 under construction. A total of 168 new reactors are expected to start up by 2020. This chart shows that the majority of those are in China and India, which are two of the most densely populated countries.

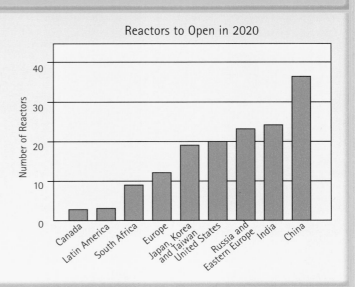

Reactors to Open in 2020

Wood—Fuel of the Poor

Figures for energy production and consumption often miss an important energy source that sustains perhaps a third of the world's population—fuelwood. Because most fuelwood is collected or traded by individuals or small groups, it does not count as commercial energy. But that does not mean it is not important. In LEDCs, wood accounts for 15 percent of the energy supply. This makes fuelwood the world's most important form of nonfossil energy.

Burning Up?

Fuelwood is used mainly by poor people in rural areas, who depend on wood fires for cooking and heating. Charcoal (produced by burning wood in a limited supply of air to make it lighter) is an important fuel among the urban poor, and is also a major industrial energy source in some Latin American countries. For example, the steel industry in Brazil depends heavily on charcoal.

Local and regional wood shortages already exist in many parts of Africa, Asia, and Latin America. These are especially likely to occur near areas of high population density, causing a "halo" of deforestation around many cities, towns, and roads. This is often open and sparse woodland, but in some cases—for example, in Thailand and Sri Lanka—closed forest can also be affected.

◀ This forest in Kerala, India, is being cleared for fuelwood.

Evidence

WORLDWIDE WOOD USAGE

You will see from the chart that more than 85 percent of wood fuel is used by Asia, South America, and Africa. Five countries—Brazil, China, India, Indonesia, and Nigeria—account for about half of the fuelwood and charcoal produced and consumed around the world each year. In some countries, such as Nepal, Uganda, Rwanda, and Tanzania, fuelwood provides 80 percent or more of the total energy requirements.

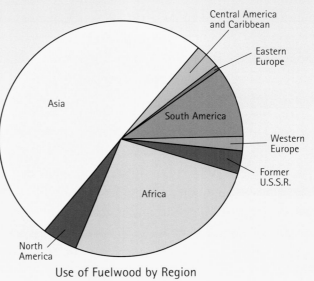

Use of Fuelwood by Region

Can it be Sustained?

Only about a third of fuelwood worldwide is taken from forests. The remainder comes from roadside verges, fallen branches, logging, and timber waste, even backyards. Some fuelwood comes from tree plantations. There is evidence to suggest that fuelwood supply in LEDCs can be sustainable—even in densely populated areas— with the help of well-managed government planting programs, community wood lots and plantations. It has been suggested, in Africa, for example, that the lack of land ownership (known as property rights) and not scarcity of trees, is often to blame for fuelwood shortages and the environmental destruction this causes. This is because locally owned plots are more likely to be cared for than government-owned or run plantations. Other evidence suggests, however, that sustainably grown wood plantations will not be able to keep pace with the growing fuel demand from a rapidly growing population.

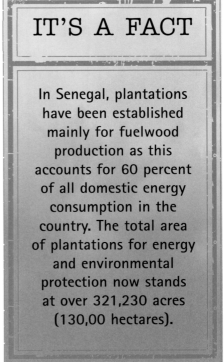

IT'S A FACT

In Senegal, plantations have been established mainly for fuelwood production as this accounts for 60 percent of all domestic energy consumption in the country. The total area of plantations for energy and environmental protection now stands at over 321,230 acres (130,00 hectares).

Growing Demand

Current patterns of energy use are one thing, but how does the picture look for the future? The economies of many non-OECD countries are growing stronger. Their GDP (Gross Domestic Product) is expected to increase by over 5 percent per year as their industry, commerce, and transportation systems become more developed. Domestic energy consumption will also rise sharply as populations increase and people demand better standards of living.

How will these increasing energy demands be met? As we have seen, reserves of oil and gas could survive the next 30 or 40 years, coal much longer. But at what price? In one year alone (2003), carbon dioxide emissions from the non-OECD countries grew by almost 10 percent, and much of this was due to a 17 percent increase in coal use in Asia. In 2004, carbon dioxide emissions from the non-OECD regions exceeded those from the OECD countries for the first time. By 2030, they could be greater by nearly 60 percent. If this happens, will the Earth survive?

▶ By the year 2050, the world's population could be around nine billion. This will mean more development like these buildings in Mumbai, India, leading to huge increases in our energy demands.

Evidence

GLOBAL ENERGY USE

This chart demonstrates how energy use is predicted to increase by nearly 60 percent between 2004 and 2030. It also shows how the increase lies largely within the non-OECD countries. Their demand for energy is growing by around 3 percent per year, but in the OECD region it is less than 1 percent. A closer look at the non-OECD countries reveals that the greatest predicted increase is in Asia—the continent that includes India and China.

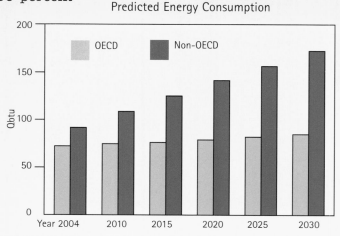

Predicted Energy Consumption

OECD   Non-OECD

Qbtu

Year 2004   2010   2015   2020   2025   2030

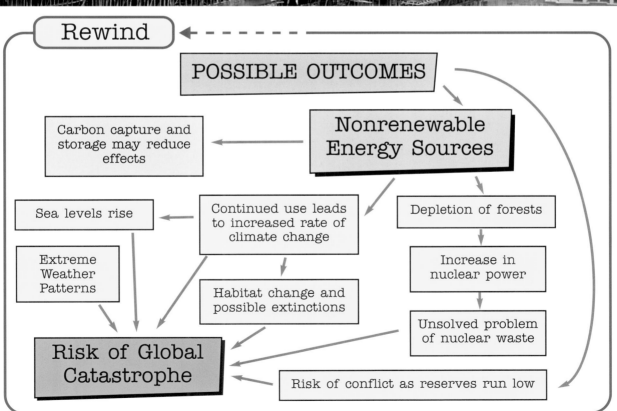

Rewind ◀ - - - - - - -

POSSIBLE OUTCOMES

Nonrenewable Energy Sources

Carbon capture and storage may reduce effects

Sea levels rise

Continued use leads to increased rate of climate change

Depletion of forests

Increase in nuclear power

Extreme Weather Patterns

Habitat change and possible extinctions

Unsolved problem of nuclear waste

Risk of Global Catastrophe

Risk of conflict as reserves run low

Sustainable Solutions

Is it possible to meet the growing global demand for energy through clean and sustainable means? This is a complex question. In order to address it, we need to look at the pros and cons of the renewable energy resources available now, those technologies that are being or could be developed—and how much of the future's energy these sources and systems might supply.

Hydropower—Water on the Move

Hydropower—energy produced by flowing water—currently provides nearly 20 percent of the world's electricity. It is seen as a low-carbon technology, once the energy-intensive building work has been completed. Hydroelectric plants, however, require large dams. These destroy the ecology of river systems by altering water flow and allowing the buildup of sediments. The accumulation of rotting organic material may produce large amounts of methane, a more powerful greenhouse gas than carbon dioxide. Dams also have

▼ This map shows the percentage of water power out of the total electricity generated by different countries around the world in 2000.

- 91–100%
- 51–90%
- 26–50%
- 11–25%
- 0–10%
- No data

enormous impact on people. Already, 40–80 million people around the world have been displaced (forced to move) by dam construction. Often, these are indigenous people who have lived in such areas for many generations.

The energy that the world could potentially achieve from hydropower is estimated to be 9–12 times current production. It is also estimated that 30 percent of this could be produced without unacceptable environmental or human impacts. Sympathetic means would involve a mixture of retrofitting older dams to make them more efficient, improving future design, and investing more in new small dams, which can serve local communities and have less impact on river systems as a whole.

Building New Dams

There are very few sites available for dam building in developed regions such as the United States and Europe. Some potential sites remain in Africa and South America, but most of the suitable locations (60 percent) are in Asia. Worldwide, 1,400 large dams are currently planned or are under construction, including 162 in northern India and a staggering 105 in the Yangtze River basin in China alone.

▼ Large dams, such as this one on the Orange River in South Africa, produce significant amounts of electrical energy, but become less efficient as silt builds up behind the dam walls.

Harnessing the Power of the Sun

Sunlight is the most abundant energy source on Earth. Present-day solar (photovoltaic) cells can convert about 15–20 percent of the sunlight that falls on them into electrical energy, and cells with much higher efficiencies are being developed. In 2005, grid-connected photovoltaic electricity was the fastest-growing renewable energy after biodiesel (see page 32)—production increased by 55 percent.

One advantage of solar cells is that they can be situated on and around existing buildings, so they do not need to take up extra space. In Germany, which is currently committed to obtaining 50 percent of its energy needs from renewable sources by 2020, a massive program is underway to fit solar cells to offices and other urban buildings. If it is successful, it is likely to be taken up by other countries.

Electrons out

Ray of light

Electrons return

Current collectors

Electrons

▲ How a photovoltaic cell works. When light energy hits the cell, it causes electrons to move from one silicon layer to the other and flow out of the circuit.

Making More of the Sun

Photovoltaic cells are not the only way of capturing the Sun's energy. It is estimated that algae farms (tanks of simple plants growing in water) could convert 10 percent of sunlight into biodiesel fuel. Roof-mounted solar thermal collectors or panels can capture 70–80 percent of the Sun's energy as usable heat—these are particularly useful in supplying hot water to homes. Other, more advanced technologies involve vast solar chimneys that suck up air warmed by the Sun, passing it over turbines to generate electricity. Huge banks of mirrors focused on boilers can perform a similar function by generating high-pressure steam.

imple solar systems have great value in ountries with poorly developed electricity grid systems and where communities may be solated. Kenya, for example, has the world's highest household solar ownership rate, with 0,000 small (20–100 watt) solar power systems sold each year.

However, solar cells work well only in direct sunlight (although this is less true of solar panels), and of course, cannot work at night. Solar cells are also expensive to make compared to the amount of electricity they produce. Locally sited, small-scale solar power, however, is likely to make an important contribution to our future energy needs.

▼ Solar cells collect the Sun's rays and convert it into electricity directly. This means that there are few energy transfers involved, making the technology efficient, but still expensive.

IT'S A FACT

It is estimated that if 1 percent of the land that is used for crops today were used for solar collection, solar power could meet the entire world's energy needs.

| 0 (0) | 4.3 (1.3) | 8.9 (2.7) | 11.5 (3.5) | 15 (4.5) | 16 (5.0) | 18 (5.5) | 19.7 (6.0) | 21.3 (6.5) | 23 (7.0) | 24.6 (7.5) | 26.2 (8.0) | 29.5 (9.0) | > 39 (12) |

Wind speed in feet (meters) per second

Catching the Wind

▲ This map shows how wind energy resources vary around the world.

Currently, about 0.5 percent of global power is generated by the wind. This could potentially rise by at least 20 or 30 times by 2020, meeting a massive 12–18 percent of the world's energy needs. The growth of wind power is currently around 25 percent per year. This is because the cost of manufacturing wind turbines has decreased rapidly as demand has grown and new generations of wind turbines are larger, more efficient, and quieter than their predecessors. The development of offshore wind farms is also becoming more viable, especially since wind power is widely seen as a realistic alternative to fossil fuels.

Like many other forms of sustainable energy, wind power is not cheap—it costs up to three times more than conventional fossil fuels per unit of energy. However, these costs are likely to continue decreasing. Today, offshore wind turbines are more expensive than onshore, but this is also likely to change.

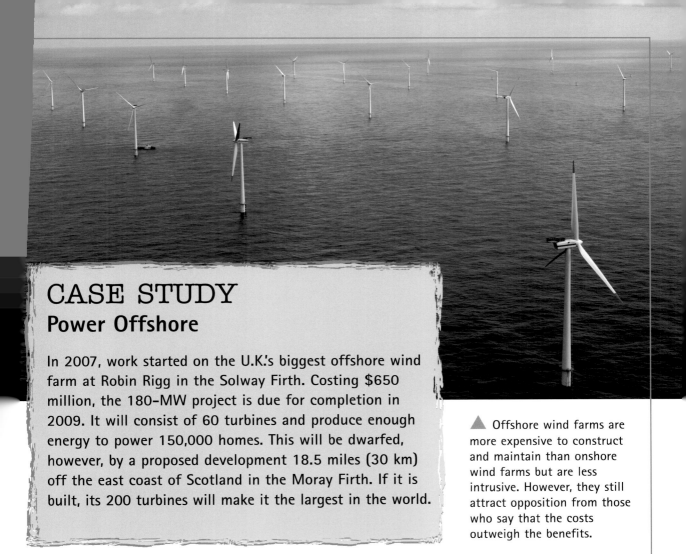

CASE STUDY
Power Offshore

In 2007, work started on the U.K.'s biggest offshore wind farm at Robin Rigg in the Solway Firth. Costing $650 million, the 180–MW project is due for completion in 2009. It will consist of 60 turbines and produce enough energy to power 150,000 homes. This will be dwarfed, however, by a proposed development 18.5 miles (30 km) off the east coast of Scotland in the Moray Firth. If it is built, its 200 turbines will make it the largest in the world.

▲ Offshore wind farms are more expensive to construct and maintain than onshore wind farms but are less intrusive. However, they still attract opposition from those who say that the costs outweigh the benefits.

Against the Odds

Wind power still attracts plenty of opposition. Much of this, usually based on noise and visual intrusion, is directed at onshore sites, especially those located or proposed near residential areas or in wild places such as national parks (where there is usually more wind). Some people believe that offshore sites may disrupt seabird nesting colonies and migration routes. Others believe that wind power is inefficient and makes little difference to carbon emissions overall. Even so, the U.K. is set to invest $20 billion in wind power by 2012. In the United States, new wind power generation is likely to exceed new nuclear build over the next decade.

IT'S A FACT

Currently, 75 percent of global wind power is produced in Europe, and most of that in just three countries—Germany, Denmark, and Spain.

Bioenergy: Living Power

Bioenergy is energy obtained from biomass (plant or animal material). This may be in the form of liquid biofuels such as biodiesel and ethanol; solid biomass such as wood or charcoal; or gases, such as methane, which are extracted when organic material (for example, urban or agricultural waste) is allowed to decompose. Globally, it is estimated that 10 percent of primary energy comes from biomass; much of this is fuelwood or charcoal.

Bioenergy is an important alternative to fossil fuels because, theoretically at least, it is carbon neutral. This means that the carbon dioxide released into the atmosphere during burning was previously removed by the plant during growth. In reality, this is rarely the case. Most biomass has to be grown, collected, or harvested and then processed into a usable form. This uses significant amounts of energy, much of it from fossil fuels.

▲ Switchgrass thrives in depleted soils and is an excellent crop for biofuel production. Many people now believe that the rush to grow biofuel crops is damaging the environment as well as causing food prices to rise.

Is There Enough Land?

There is also concern that crops, such as corn and sugar cane, grown for fuel will displace conventional food crops in areas where food is already in short supply. Important habitats such as grasslands, forests, and wetlands may come under increasing pressure, too, as the need to find land to grow alternative energy sources increases. This criticism has already been leveled at Brazil, where large areas of forest have been cleared to grow sugar cane for ethanol production.

IT'S A FACT

The Worldwatch Institute estimates that producing 10 percent of the world's transportation fuels from crops would require 9 percent of the planet's agricultural land.

CASE STUDY
Bioethanol—Friend or Foe?

▲ At this bioethanol plant in the U.S.A., corn is processed to produce fuel.

The United States, among other countries, has turned to making bioethanol from corn as a replacement for some of its massive use of gasoline. A number of recent studies, however, suggest that producing bioethanol from corn barely reduces the overall carbon footprint compared to using conventional fossil fuels. Materials left over after processing, however, such as stems, husks, and leaves, are often high in protein and can be used as animal feed or natural composts, reducing the need for manufactured feeds and fertilizers.

There may be a better alternative in cellulosic ethanol. This is bioethanol produced from nonfood sources, such as prairie grasses and woody plants. Cellulosic ethanol reduces emissions by 87 percent compared to gasoline. This type of cultivation may also be better suited to the needs of wildlife.

Geothermal Energy: Energy From Below

Geothermal energy is used commercially in more than 70 countries. It draws on the heat in underground rocks to heat water, which can be used either directly or turned into steam that drives turbines for electricity generation. Currently, commercial geothermal energy supplies a tiny 0.25 percent of total global energy consumption—but this increases to almost 0.75 percent when ground source heat pumps are included (see page 35). Because geothermal energy draws heat from rocks, it is not renewable in the same sense as solar energy, for example.

Digging Deep

Geothermal heat is close to the Earth's surface only in certain parts of the world; the five top geothermal energy producers—the United States, the Philippines,

▲ This geothermal plant is in Kenya. Since geothermal energy draws on underground heat, it is less intrusive than many other technologies. However, it still has an envionmental impact.

> ## IT'S A FACT
>
> A country like Iceland— which heats 86 percent of all its houses using geothermal energy—could sustain its current level of consumption for at least another 1,200 years.

Mexico, Italy, and Indonesia—are good examples. Elsewhere, energy can potentially be generated from deeper under the ground using a process called hot dry rock technology. Holes at least 1.9 miles (3 kilometers) deep are drilled into the earth. Water is pumped into some of the holes, where it is heated by the hot rock, and then pumped out of others. Australia is currently exploring the technology necessary to make this commercially viable.

Pros and Cons

Large-scale geothermal energy is expensive and not without other problems. Although there are few emissions, solid material brought up with the water may be toxic or even radioactive, and has to be disposed of. The liquids themselves can be corrosive, causing damage to pipework and machinery. Where boreholes have been sunk in some places to tap into hot, underground water, natural hot water springs nearby have been disrupted. However, despite these drawbacks and the many technical difficulties that exist, the potential of geothermal energy remains almost limitless.

CASE STUDY
Ground Source Heat Pumps

Ground source heat pumps (GSHPs) use low-level heat in the ground and "upgrade" this into usable heat. They act something like refrigerators but in reverse. A long loop of pipe is buried in the ground and filled with a mixture of water and antifreeze (refrigerant). The refrigerant extracts heat from the ground and passes through an evaporator, where it becomes a gas. This is then compressed by a pump, which raises its temperature to the level required by the house. Finally, the vaporized refrigerant passes through a condenser that releases the heat into water that can be used to warm the house or contribute to the hot water system.

Although GSHPs use electricity to drive the pump and compressor, this energy is returned three- or four-fold by the device. One advantage is that GSHPs can be fitted to individual houses, as long as there is sufficient surrounding area for the ground loop. GSHPs are gaining acceptance in the United States and Europe, with more than 66,000 installed annually worldwide.

Sea Power

There are many ways in which the energy contained in the movement of the sea can be harnessed. Wave power uses the energy in waves to drive floating structures, or pontoons, up and down and convert this movement into electrical energy. Tidal power captures energy from the up and down motion of the tides. A barrier or barrage is built in a basin, such as an estuary or other inlet. This traps the rising water when the tide comes in. Around low tide, the water in the basin is discharged through turbines, generating electricity from the kinetic energy released.

Making Waves

In 2006, Portugal built the world's first commercial "wave farm." It is capable of generating 2.25 MW—enough to supply 1,500 homes. If the project proves successful, more wave machines will be built, giving a total capacity of 72 MW and occupying 0.4 square miles (1 sq km) of ocean. In 2007, the construction of a wave farm began in Orkney, off the north coast of Scotland.

IT'S A FACT

The north and south temperate zones (above and below the tropics) have the best sites for capturing wave power. The prevailing westerly winds (which generate waves) in these zones blow strongest here, especially in winter.

CASE STUDY
A Daring Plan?

One possible site for a tidal barrage is the Severn Estuary in southwest England. If it is built, the barrier would span the entire estuary 10 miles (16 km) and have an energy capacity of nearly 9,000 MW, which is enough to supply 12 percent of the United Kingdom's electricity. The drawbacks are severe, however. They include obstructions to shipping and fish migration, and dramatic disruption to the estuary's mudflats between high and low tides. This in turn would have grave consequences for the 63,000 wading birds that use the mudflats for feeding. In addition, much of the waste flowing down the estuary would be trapped for longer periods of time, seriously polluting a 1,275-sq-mi. (3,300-sq-km) body of water behind the barrier. Objectors say there are less damaging ways of using the Severn's 40-ft. (12-m) tidal range, including "stand-alone" tidal generators, tidal fences, and tidal lagoons.

Riding the Tide

The technical and environmental problems connected with tidal barrages are considerable. This may explain why there are currently only two large-scale tidal capture plants operating commercially in the world—one at St. Malo in the northwest of France (240 MW) and one in Nova Scotia, Canada (16 MW). There is also a lack of suitable sites, because a large tidal range (the vertical distance for which the tide moves) is required.

Underwater Windmills

Tidal stream power captures the energy from the flow of tides, rather than from their vertical movement. To do this, underwater structures resembling wind turbines are usually used. Although this kind of energy capture is currently mainly at the development stage, the first commercial 1.2 MW prototype (test model) was installed in March 2008 in Strangford Lough, Northern Ireland. Its makers claim that future underwater turbines could supply 10 percent of the United Kingdom's energy, depending on what impact the turbines have on marine life.

▼ Arrays of underwater turbines like this may look futuristic, but they are serious contenders as future renewable energy sources; as with other new energy sources, however, high construction costs and lack of suitable sites may hamper the development of this technology.

Doing More with Less: Energy Efficiency and Conservation

There is plenty of technology already available that can increase the efficiency with which people use and save energy. Low-energy light bulbs, more efficient appliances, and better insulation are all important examples. Heat exchangers make it possible to recover some of the energy in waste warm water and air to heat incoming fresh water or air. Existing power plants can undergo fairly minor modifications to reduce their energy wastage, and new power plants can benefit from what is called cogeneration, or combined heat and power. This means the waste heat from the steam used to turn turbines is "recycled" to heat local homes and offices.

▲ Hybrid cars like this one improve the efficiency of gasoline transportation by converting "wasted" energy from braking into electricity.

Transportation

Some of the greatest energy savings to be made are in transportation. Mass transportation systems (bus and train, for example) are more efficient than conventional cars. Cars themselves now consume less fuel, because they are made of lighter materials and have more efficient engines. Hybrid vehicles, which run partly on fuel and partly on electricity, will be more efficient still by regaining the energy used in braking to charge batteries that can power the car at low speeds or when idling in traffic. Eventually, vehicles may run on hydrogen rather than gas or diesel, using fuel cell technology (see page 43).

Efficient Buildings

In many parts of the world, tougher building regulations mean that modern buildings are much more energy efficient than those built in the past. Many countries are moving toward "carbon neutral" buildings, in which the energy used in construction is offset (balanced out) by energy conservation measures, renewable energy use, or carbon-capturing projects such as planting trees. Many new building designs will incorporate techniques such as "passive solar", meaning they will take advantage of natural heat and light from the Sun through use of special materials and careful siting.

Better Distribution

Electricity distribution may also change in the future. Large-scale (national) grids waste energy as heat, as the electrical current passes through many miles of wire. Small-scale, often renewable, energy sources will be placed closer to users so that less energy is lost during transmission. This so-called distributed energy means that individuals and small communities who are generating their own electricity, for example, through solar cells, can sell surplus power back to the grid.

CASE STUDY
Introducing the Carbon-Neutral Country!

Costa Rica, in Central America, aims to be fully carbon neutral before 2030. In 2004, nearly 50 percent of the country's primary energy came from renewable sources; within this, 94 percent of all electricity was generated from hydroelectric power, wind farms, and geothermal energy. The government imposes a 3.5 percent tax on gasoline, and the revenue is used to make payments that encourage landowners to grow trees and protect forests.

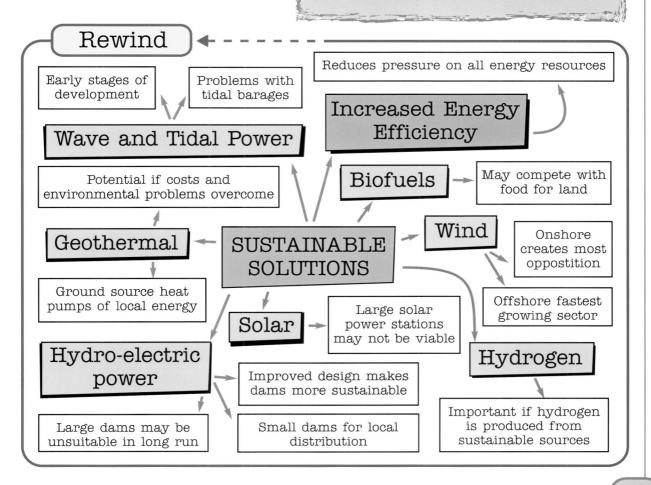

What the Future Holds

It is clear that providing and distributing energy in a changing world is not a straightforward matter. While it seems obvious that a reduction in the use of fossil fuels and a switch to renewable power is sensible, in reality this holds many complications. So how do things look for the future?

Looking Ahead

It is important to look at the factors that "drive" sustainable energy technologies, in order to see how they might make a greater contribution to the future energy mix. Currently, most renewable energy is more expensive than conventional energy supplies (discounting the environmental costs). Will the world find a way to make renewables pay?

Evidence

IN THE FUTURE?

This table gives figures for current use and "technical potential" of the main renewable energy sources. Technical potential is what is possible using current or developing technologies. The figures give only a theoretical idea of what might be achieved at some point in the future. For example, the target for geothermal energy is very high— obtaining even a small proportion of it would require engineering on a scale that is unlikely to occur.

ENERGY TYPE	CURRENT USE	TECHNICAL POTENTIAL
Hydropower	9	50
Biomass (including wood)	50	275
Solar energy	0.1	1,575
Wind energy	0.12	640
Geothermal energy	0.6	5,000
Ocean energy	low	not estimated
TOTAL	60	7,600

Figures are in so-called exajoules per year.
For comparison, current annual global energy use is about 400 exajoules.

▲ In the right location, solar cells and solar heating panels can make a real contribution to meeting future energy needs.

Giving Renewables a Chance

Primarily, renewable energy needs to become more competitive. Financial support from governments can accelerate development and allow technologies to take hold in what is known as the energy market. This may involve government grants for research into cheaper and better systems, loans, tax subsidies, or rebates (repayments) to those who buy the type of energy concerned.

It is also possible to make fossil fuels less competitive by taxing them more. The revenue (income) earned from so-called carbon taxes can be channeled toward renewable energy development and so reduce carbon emissions.

An International Response?

Many people argue that an overall, international drive is needed to create a competitive renewable energy "infrastructure". For example, the MEDCs could invest more in research and development, and manufacturing could be transferred to LEDCs where costs are often lower. Even this will not happen unless private companies recognize that renewable energy is the next "big industry" and invest heavily in the technology. There is evidence that some companies, such as British Petroleum (BP), are beginning to do this.

Storing Energy

Costs are not the only factor that will affect the future of new technologies. One of the problems associated with renewable energy is that it is intermittent, or variable—for example, neither wind nor solar energy is available all the time—so it is not always possible to match the supply with the demand. Better storage methods are required to make energy available when it is needed. There are a number of ways of doing this. Pumped-storage hydroelectric systems, for example, use excess energy to pump water back to a higher level where its stored (potential) energy can be used when required. Spare or excess energy capacity can also be used to produce hydrogen from water and then used later in fuel cells or burned directly (see page 43).

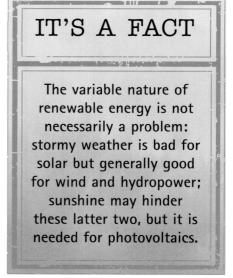

IT'S A FACT

The variable nature of renewable energy is not necessarily a problem: stormy weather is bad for solar but generally good for wind and hydropower; sunshine may hinder these latter two, but it is needed for photovoltaics.

Land Grabbers?

Other objections to renewable energy sources include their unsightly appearance (especially in the case of wind turbines) or their use of valuable land (in the case of bioethanol, in particular). Sometimes, it is a case of finding the right technology for the right situation. Fixed solar arrays, for example, can double as noise barriers along highways or they can be used to clad office buildings. Amorphous (transparent) photovoltaic cells can be employed simultaneously to tint windows on buildings and produce electricity.

The issue of using more land for growing biofuels rather than food is still unresolved, as is the damage caused to natural habitats by increasing biofuel production. Of course, it has to be remembered that fossil fuel extraction can also be damaging to land, particularly the recent practice of stripping large areas for so-called oil sands (clay and sand deposits containing high levels of bitumen from which oil can be extracted). In the end, however, difficult decisions will need to be made, and of course, many other renewable technologies, such as wind power, can usually take place with little effect on an area's biodiversity or agricultural value.

CASE STUDY
Sustainable Cells

A significant advance in energy storage is the development of fuel cells that use hydrogen to produce electricity. Hydrogen can be obtained by splitting water, which is made up of hydrogen and oxygen, in a process that requires electricity itself. If this electricity is obtained from a renewable source (say a wind turbine working at peak capacity), the surplus energy can be captured and stored in the chemical bonds of the hydrogen molecules. The advantage of this system is that hydrogen can be used in motor vehicles and other forms of transportation. Because transportation is the fastest-growing sector, the widespread introduction of fuel cell technology could do much to reduce the world's dependence on fossil fuels and eliminate a huge source of global pollution.

▼ Fuel cells can reduce pollution in cities by using hydrogen obtained from other renewable energy sources.

Can the World Survive?

In May 2007, the World Wildlife Fund (WWF) put forward an alternative strategy for meeting the world's energy demands. This proposed some strikingly different solutions to most current scenarios in which both fossil fuels and nuclear power continue to play the dominant role.

Some regions, notably the European Union (EU), can work to agree targets that will reduce dependency on fossil fuels. Currently the EU members have agreed to an overall aim of generating 20 percent of their energy through renewables by the year 2020.

But what about LEDCs? It is easy to criticize countries such as China and India, with their growing demand for energy, but they have not had the benefits of industrialization that MEDCs have enjoyed for several hundred years. This does not mean the world can afford to let these countries develop in the same way. But it does mean MEDCs should help them to achieve more appropriate energy strategies, including greater access to renewables.

▶ China is already taking action to help reduce the threat of energy shortages and global warming. It currently has more small hydroelectric dams than anywhere else in the world. It is also home to the massive Three Gorges dam, shown here.

Evidence

PROJECTED ENERGY SUPPLY

This simplified version of the WWF's projections suggests that the biggest contributions could be made by energy efficiency and conservation. Renewables could meet 70 percent of the remaining demand. The figures also imply that fossil fuels will continue to play an important role, assuming that carbon capture and storage (CCS) occurs (see page 19). In this scenario, there is no long-term future for nuclear power.

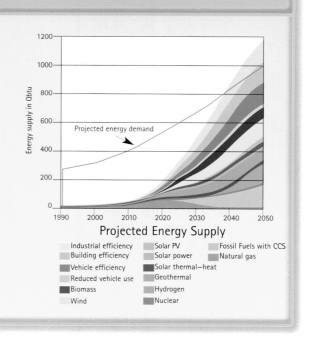

Projected Energy Supply

Projected energy demand

Industrial efficiency	Solar PV	Fossil Fuels with CCS
Building efficiency	Solar power	Natural gas
Vehicle efficiency	Solar thermal—heat	
Reduced vehicle use	Geothermal	
Biomass	Hydrogen	
Wind	Nuclear	

Making a Difference

Is the world running out of energy? The answer is no—energy is all around us. The real question is: how can this energy be obtained without seriously damaging the planet that provides us with so much of it? One answer is that people have to recognize they are a global society. *Global citizenship* is when individuals recognize they are all citizens of the same world; that their actions have an impact on the rest of the planet. Accepting this interdependence also means accepting responsibility to make changes, both at an individual level and at a national and international level. Everyone can make small changes by using less energy in their everyday lives. People need to be aware of the bigger picture, however. The energy future of this planet concerns everyone.

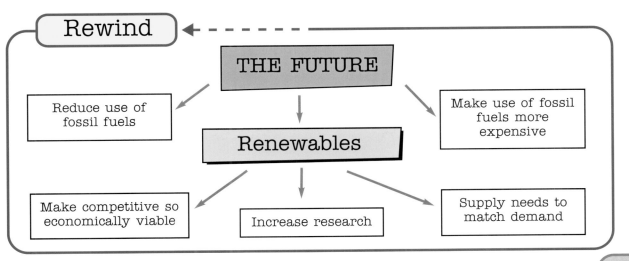

Rewind

THE FUTURE

Reduce use of fossil fuels

Renewables

Make use of fossil fuels more expensive

Make competitive so economically viable

Increase research

Supply needs to match demand

Glossary, Further Information, and Web Sites

Antifreeze Liquid that is added to water to lower its freezing point.

Biodiversity The variety of plants and animals.

Biofuel Fuel made from plants grown on plantations, agricultural by-products, or domestic or agricultural waste.

Carbon footprint A measure of the quantity of emissions caused by an activity or the manufacturing of a product.

Carbon tax A tax that raises income to invest in more sustainable energy production.

Closed forest Forest with continuous tree cover.

Commercial energy Energy that is bought and sold.

Corrosive Any strong chemical compound, such as an acid, which has a damaging effect on materials or living tissue.

Fuelwood Wood used primarily for heat or for conversion to other forms of energy.

GDP Gross Domestic Product— how much a country earns from all its industrial, manufacturing, and commercial activities.

Grid A means of national or regional distribution, applied to transmission of electricity.

Infrastructure The buildings, transportation systems, communications, and services that support an area.

Megawatt hour (MWh) 1,000 kilowatt hours (kWh).

Nonrenewable resources Energy or other resources that are not replaced (or renewed) as they are being used.

Primary energy The energy in raw fuels that has not been part of a conversion process.

Reactor core The part of a nuclear reactor in which nuclear fission (splitting of atoms) takes place and that generates huge quantities of heat energy.

Renewable resources Energy or other resources that do not run out with use.

Slag heaps Piles of waste resulting from the extraction of minerals.

Sustainable Carried out without depleting or permanently damaging resources.

Books to read

Fossil Fuels
Conrad J Storad (Lerner Publications, 2007)

Issues of the World: Energy Crisis
Ewan McLeish (Stargazer, 2007)

Science Files, Energy: Oil and Gas
Steve Parker (Gareth Stevens Publishing, 2004)

The Pros and Cons of Solar Power
Isabel Thomas (Rosen, 2007)

The Pros and Cons of Wind Power
Richard and Louise Spilsbury (Rosen, 2007)

Web Sites

Due to the changing nature of Internet links, Rosen Publishing has developed an online list of Web sites related to the subject of this book. This site is regularly updated. Please use this link to access this list: www.rosenlinks.com/ces/ener

Topic Web

Use this topic web to discover themes and ideas in subjects that are related to energy sources.

English and Literacy

- Debate the pros and cons of increasing nuclear power capacity as a replacement for fossil fuels.
- How energy issues are dealt with in movies and fiction.
- Read accounts of people who have lost their livelihoods through the collapse of the coal industry or lost relatives in mining accidents.

History and Economics

- Development of different energy sources in a historical context.
- Conflicts arising out of the need for greater "energy security" as fossil fuel reserves decrease, for example, the Iraq wars.
- Relative costs of different energy sources, including the "hidden costs," for example, of decommissioning nuclear power stations.

Science and Environment

- Pros and cons of different energy sources and their applications.
- Understanding different types of energy and energy transfers.
- Units of energy and power and the cost of electricity.
- Environmental issues related to the extraction, transportation, and production of energy resources.
- Evidence for global climate change.

Energy

Art and Culture

- Mining in a culture and the effect on that culture following the closure of mines.
- Mining and industry in art, e.g. works by L.S. Lowry.
- Loss of culture due to movement of whole communities as a result of dam building and flooding of large areas of land.

Geography

- Distribution of energy resources.
- Energy trading and transportation.
- Extraction technologies.
- Effects of global warming on habitats and human populations.
- Sustainable energy and future energy sources.

Index

Contents

Tornadoes Are a Deadly Disaster

A tornado is a twirling column of air stretching down from a thunderstorm to the ground. Tornadoes can cause major destruction. They can damage or destroy homes and property in just minutes. Tornadoes can also cause injury or death to people and animals caught in their path.

The path of destruction left by a tornado can vary in size. The largest and most powerful tornadoes may leave a path about 1 mile (1.6 kilometers) wide and up to 50 miles (80 km) long. In the United States, damage from tornadoes leads to about 1,500 injuries and 70 deaths each year. Tornadoes mostly take place during spring and summer in North America. Most tornadoes happen either in Florida or in the southern **plains** of central United States.

The path of damage caused by a tornado is usually less than 1,600 feet (500 meters) wide.

A tornado may appear almost completely transparent, or see-through, until it either picks up dust and debris or a cloud forms inside the funnel.

Tornadoes Are Caused by Warm and Cold Air Mixing Together

Tornadoes form when warm, moist air meets cold, dry air. This happens when cold air pushes the warm air down. However, warm air is lighter than cold air. This makes the warm air rise back up through the cold air. The rising warm air is called an updraft.

TYPES OF TORNADOS

Dust Devils	**Dust Devils** are a type of whirlwind. Whirlwinds are weaker than tornadoes and fairly short-lived. Dust devils form in the desert when light winds create a whirlwind of dust. They are harmless and usually do not reach speeds of more than 25 miles (49 km) an hour.
Firewhirls	**Firewhirls** are sometimes formed by forest fires or volcano eruptions. A rotating column of fire or smoke forms with speeds of more than 100 miles (160 km) per hour. Firewhirls are sometimes called fire tornadoes.
Gustnadoes	**Gustnadoes** are brief dust or debris clouds that form along a thunderstorm front. They only reach heights of 30 to 300 feet (9 to 90 m) above the ground. Gustnadoes do not connect to storm clouds higher in the sky the way tornadoes do. Wind speeds range from 60 to 80 miles (100 to 130 km) an hour.
Landspouts	**Landspouts** form beneath cumulus clouds like waterspouts on land.
Supercell Tornadoes	**Supercell Tornadoes** are the strongest type of tornadoes. They form from supercell thunderstorms. These are long storms that have constantly rotating updrafts of air. Supercell tornadoes have wind speeds of more than 65 miles (105 km) per hour.
Waterspouts	**Waterspouts** are like tornadoes. They occur when a funnel forms over the warm tropical ocean. They usually dissolve when they reach land.

If the speed or direction of the wind changes, the updraft begins to turn. As the updraft turns, it sucks in more warm, moist air. Bringing in more warm air makes the updraft stronger and causes the air to turn even faster. Drops of water from the moist updraft then form a **funnel cloud**. This funnel grows and extends toward the ground. It continues to grow until it touches the ground. When the funnel cloud touches the ground, it becomes a tornado.

Though tornadoes can appear at any time, they are most likely to form between 3 PM and 9 PM.

Tornados Cannot Be Prevented

Though tornadoes cannot be prevented, there are things people can do to be safe. Sometimes, tornadoes strike without warning. There may not even be a nearby thunderstorm. Many times, however, there are signs that a tornado could be about to form. These signs include a dark and stormy sky, dark clouds hanging low in the **atmosphere**, large hail stones, or a loud sound like an oncoming train.

It is important for people to know what to do if they see a tornado or hear a tornado warning. People that live in areas that are known to have tornadoes should make a tornado emergency plan. All family members should know where to take shelter when a tornado strikes.

Tornado winds are strong enough to pick up a house and carry it to the next block.

One of the safest places to take shelter is in the middle of a basement.

In homes and buildings without basements, people should go to a room with no windows on the ground level. This could include a closet, a bathroom, or a hallway. Keep charged batteries on hand to listen to the radio, computer, or television for updates on the storm.

Most tornado warnings only give people 13 minutes to take shelter. Nearly 70 percent of these warnings are false alarms.

There are other steps people can take to make sure their homes or places of business are prepared for a tornado. Furniture should be pushed away from windows, and emergency food and water should be stored in a safe place.

Some people believe that leaving windows open during a tornado will prevent damage to their homes. This is not true. If a window is left open, it will allow air to rush into the house. The house may then be blown apart from the inside.

Tornadoes Happen Around the World

All continents have reported tornadoes except Antarctica. They take place most often in places where cold polar air and warm tropical air meet. The United States has more tornadoes than any other country in the world. Each year, more than 1,000 tornadoes take place in the United States. Of those, 10 to 20 tornadoes are strong enough to cause severe damage.

The violent tornadoes that occur in the United States are not reported as often in other countries. Canada reports the next highest **frequency** of tornadoes, with 80 to 100 per year. When measuring tornadoes by size of the country, Great Britain has the most. There are an average of 33 tornadoes reported there each year, but most of them are weak.

In order for a twisting column of air to be ranked as a tornado, it must remain in contact with the cloud above and the ground below.

Tornadoes also happen in South Africa, Bangladesh, Uruguay, Russia, and Australia. Russia and Australia are very large countries. Some parts of these countries do not have any people living there. This makes it difficult to know how many tornadoes actually take place in these parts of the world.

Most tornadoes travel from the southwest to the northeast, but they can reverse if they are hit by winds from the eye of a thunderstorm.

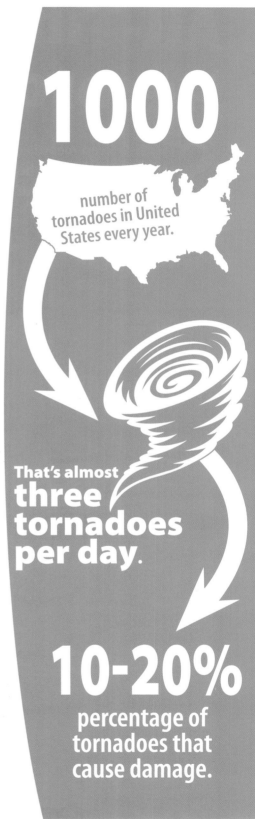

1000
number of tornadoes in United States every year.

That's almost **three tornadoes per day**.

10-20%
percentage of tornadoes that cause damage.

All-Time Records

Scientists keep records of tornadoes. They collect information and study patterns in the weather. This helps them know when a tornado may be about to form. They can then sent out a tornado warning to the people living in the area.

DEADLIEST

The deadliest tornado in the United States was the "Tri-State" tornado on March 18, 1925. It created a 219-mile (352-km) long track as it raged across parts of Missouri, Illinois, and Indiana. It caused the deaths of 695 people.

BIGGEST

The biggest known deadly tornado was on May 31, 2013, near El Reno, Oklahoma. It left a path 2.6-miles. (4.2-km) wide.

COSTLIEST

The costliest recorded tornado happened on May 22, 2011, in Joplin, Missouri. The damage was estimated at $2.8 billion.

MOST TORNADOES IN A MONTH

April 2011 set the record for most tornadoes in a single month. That month, 817 tornadoes took place across the United States.

Tornadoes in the United States

Most tornadoes in the United States happen in Tornado Alley which is in the south central part of the United States. Tornado Alley spans Alabama, Arkansas, Florida, Georgia, Illinois, Indiana, Iowa, Kansas, Louisiana, Mississippi, Missouri, Nebraska, Oklahoma, South Dakota, and Texas. Warm, moist air that comes off the Gulf of Mexico collides with drier, cold air that comes from Canada to create tornadoes.

AVERAGE NUMBER OF TORNADOS PER YEAR

0–5	
6–20	
21–40	
41–60	
61–80	
81–150	

Pacific Ocean

MAP SCALE

0   500 miles

500 kilometers

North Dakota

Minnesota

South Dakota

Nebraska

Kansas

Oklahoma

Texas

Wisconsin

Iowa

Missouri

Arkansas

Louisiana

Illinois

Indiana

Michigan

Ohio

Kentucky

Tennessee

Mississippi

Alabama

Georgia

Florida

West Virginia

Virginia

North Carolina

South Carolina

Pennsylvania

New York

Lake Superior

Lake Huron

Lake Michigan

Lake Erie

Lake Ontario

New Hampshire

Vermont

Maine

Massachusetts

Rhode Island

Connecticut

New Jersey

Delaware

Maryland

Atlantic Ocean

Gulf of Mexico

Tornado Chasers Follow these Deadly Storms to Study Them

A tornado chaser is a person who drives a special vehicle, called a Tornado Interceptor Vehicle, into a storm. The goal is to research the storms and help keep people safe. Storm chasing is especially popular in Tornado Alley because of the high number of tornadoes that take place there.

Storm chasers work to learn how a storm has developed, where it is going, and how severe it will be. Most storm chasers study weather information in science journals, books, and weather reports to find out how where they may form. Many of the people who chase storms are professional **meteorologists**.

Tornadoes are not the only danger faced by tornado chasers. They must also be careful of the lightning from the thunderstorms that often accompany tornadoes.

John Muir is thought to be one of the first storm chasers. He wanted to know what the tops of trees feel in the middle of a storm. In December 1874, Muir decided to find out by climbing a 100-foot (30-m) tall Douglas spruce in the Sierra region of California. He stayed there for hours, hanging on to the top of the tree until the storm passed.

Roger Jensen hunted for severe weather, storms, and tornadoes in the late 1940s. David Hoadley has been doing similar work since 1956. He is called the **pioneer** storm chaser.

Storm chasing is a very dangerous activity. Tornadoes may change direction suddenly and head toward the storm chasers. There is also a risk of being hit by lightning or large hail stones. Though it is rare, storm chasers have died in their line of work. To improve their safety, storm chasers usually travel in pairs. One person follows the weather reports and the other communicates with other chasers by phone or radio.

In the southern United States, most tornado chasers park to the southeast of a tornado. It is the safest spot from which they can record the tornado.

Joplin, Missouri
May 22, 2011

200-mile (320-km) per hour winds

162 people died

$2.8 billion in damage

More than 17,000 people affected

Dr. Tetsuya Theodore Fujita created the Fujita Scale

In many parts of the world, tornado strength is measured using the Fujita Scale, or F-Scale, created by Dr. Tetsuya Theodore Fujita. The F-Scale system measures the intensity of a tornado based on the severity of damage to buildings and plant life. The F-Scale has six levels. An F0 tornado is the weakest, while an F5 is the strongest. Each level of the scale is divided by wind speeds. However, these speeds are only estimates because it is too dangerous to measure the ground wind speeds or a tornado.

Dr. Tetsuya Theodore Fujita was a Japanese-American meteorologist. Fujita was one of the most respected storm researchers in the world. He studied hurricanes, tornadoes, typhoons, and severe thunderstorms both in Japan and at the University of Chicago. His many breakthroughs in people's understanding of how tornadoes work earned him the nickname Mr. Tornado.

Storm chasers use computers to help them track storms and determine where they fit on the F-Scale.

In 2007, the Enhanced Fujita Scale, or E-F Scale, replaced the F-Scale in all tornado damage surveys in the United States. Like the F-Scale, the E-F Scale also uses the numbers zero to five to measure the strength of tornadoes. However, the E-F Scale tries to provide a more accurate guide to how much property damage each level of tornado may cause.

Enhanced Fujita Scale

EF0	65-85 miles (104–137 km) per hour	Light damage. Some damage to chimneys; branches broken off trees; shallow-rooted trees pushed over; sign boards damaged.
EF1	86–110 miles (138–177 km) per hour	Moderate damage. Roofs peeled off, mobile homes overturned, or pushed off their foundations, cars blown off streets.
EF2	111–135 miles (178–217 km) per hour	Considerable damage. Roofs torn off frame houses; mobile homes demolished; boxcars overturned; large trees snapped or uprooted; light-object missiles generated; cars lifted off ground.
EF3	136–165 miles (218–266 km) per hour	Severe damage. Roofs and some walls torn off well-constructed houses; trains overturned; most trees in forest uprooted; heavy cars lifted off the ground and thrown.
EF4	166–200 miles (267–322 km) per hour	Devastating damage. Well-constructed homes levelled; other weaker buildings structures blown away; vehicles thrown and large objects hurled like missiles.
EF5	200 miles (322 km) per hour or higher	Incredible damage. Houses swept off foundations and thrown away, large objects (such as vehicles) thrown in the air 100 yards or more, bark of trees peeled off.

Little Known Facts

LOOK IN THE TREES

After a tornado has passed, people often find trees with objects such as knives and forks stuck into them.

TORNADO CENTRAL

About 75 percent of all tornadoes that take place around the world happen in the United States.

SKIPPING TWISTER

Tornadoes will sometimes 'hop'. When this happens, a tornado can destroy one house but leave the house next door completely untouched.

STRONGEST WINDS

The wind of a tornado is the strongest wind on Earth. Even hurricanes and typhoons do not reach the extremely high wind speeds of the strongest tornadoes.

TRAIN TOSS

In 1931, a tornado in Mississippi picked up an 83 ton (75 metric ton) train and tossed it about 80 feet (24 m) away.

The Center of a Tornado Is Called the Eye

The eye of a tornado is at the **epicenter** of the funnel. At the center, the air is somewhat calm. It is an area where there is low pressure. The calm air is sucked down by the low pressure. An ring, called an annulus, forms around the eye when low pressure at the bottom sucks air from the top down. When the air arrives at the bottom, it meets incoming air. This causes the upward spiral in an annulus.

HOW AIR MOVES THROUGH A TORNADO

Warm, hot air rises through the funnel cloud of the tornado while cold, damp air falls through the epicenter.

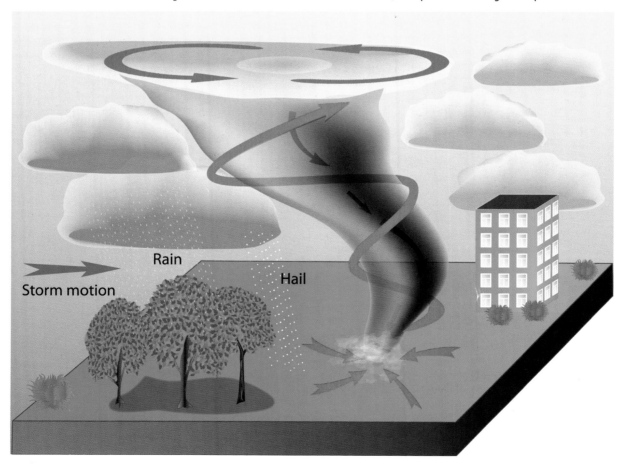

Rain

Hail

Storm motion

In the eye of a tornado, air moves in a counterclockwise direction. The eye of a tornado is only a few feet (m) in diameter. A tornado's center is chaotic. The funnel clouds are continuously moving. There is no perfect calm place in the epicenter.

A rotating thunderstorm, or mesocyclone, is one of the best predictors of tornado activity.

Hurricanes, Cyclones, and typhoons Are Like Very Large Tornadoes

Tornados are powerful storms that take place on land and cover a small area. Similar storms that happen on the water with low pressure systems and high winds are called hurricanes, cyclones, and typhoons. They are all similar with different degrees of danger and damage. They have different names specific to the part of the world where the storms take place.

Satellites flying high above Earth can spot hurricanes as they form. They look like large clouds spiraling in toward the center.

For these storms to happen, they need warm water of about 80 °Fahrenheit (27 °Celsius) or higher. These massive storms take place in a low pressure areas where warm and cool air mix. These types of storms usually die out when they reach land. If the conditions are just right, they may turn into tornadoes on land.

OTHER TYPES OF DISASTERS

Cyclone

A cyclone develops a **closed circulation**. This is when winds blow around a center. The storm rotates in a counterclockwise in the northern **hemisphere** and clockwise in the southern hemisphere.

Hurricane

A hurricane has wind speeds higher than 74 miles (119 km) an hour. They happen in the Atlantic and Northeast Pacific Oceans. Hurricanes have tremendous power and are capable of widespread destruction.

Typhoon

A typhoon is a severe tropical storm. Cyclones and typhoons take place in the Northwest Pacific Ocean. Typhoons are often stronger than hurricanes because the storm forms in open water. This creates a larger and stronger storm.

American Indian Myths Tell About Where Tornadoes Come From

There are many ancient myths and legends about how tornadoes came to be. This is an ancient Oklahoma legend.

According to an ancient Oklahoma legend, a community shunned a Indian youth because he had a very bad temper. He did not try to control his temper. He hurt and destroyed whatever came in his path when he was angry. The **elders** thought he should be sent away from the village. Even the medicine man's herbs and practices did not help stop the youth's anger. Finally the elders decided that the boy should be locked up. They built a strong prison and locked him in.

Since the boy had nothing else to do, he swirled in his prison cell. He built up more anger as he circled. Soon, he looked like a cloud of dust. The prison walls burst from the pressure, and the circling boy was free. He laughed at the people who had put him in prison and said, "You will be sorry." He jumped high in the sky and came back down, destroying people and places in his village. Wherever he touched down, he left a path of destruction.

The boy's mother cried to the Creator for help. As she cried, her tears fell on a lizard. As the lizard caught the tears, he said, "Although his anger cannot be controlled completely, the Creator will hold onto him for most of the year. He will only be released during the season of growth, the spring and summer. Each spring the twisting swirling youth made his way back destroying whatever he touched.

The lizard taught the people how to protect themselves and fewer people died. The tornado continues today. The Creator holds tightly onto the boy but finally he breaks free to dance around on the earth destroying what comes in his path. His name is tornado.

Tornado Timeline

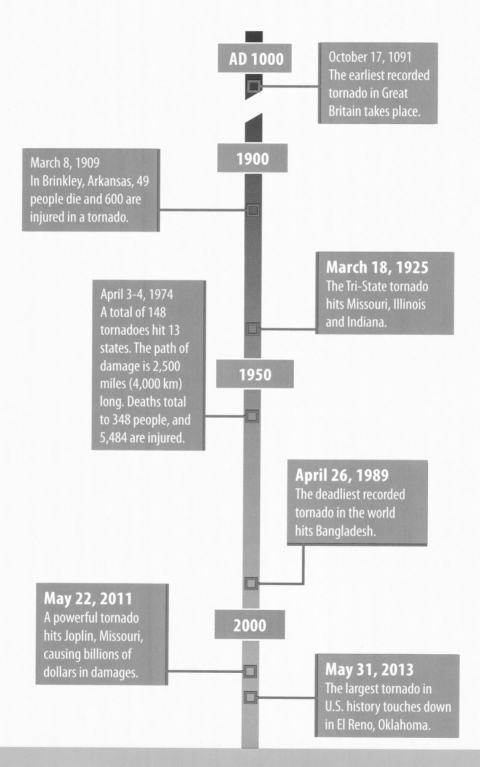

AD 1000

October 17, 1091
The earliest recorded tornado in Great Britain takes place.

1900

March 8, 1909
In Brinkley, Arkansas, 49 people die and 600 are injured in a tornado.

March 18, 1925
The Tri-State tornado hits Missouri, Illinois and Indiana.

April 3-4, 1974
A total of 148 tornadoes hit 13 states. The path of damage is 2,500 miles (4,000 km) long. Deaths total to 348 people, and 5,484 are injured.

1950

April 26, 1989
The deadliest recorded tornado in the world hits Bangladesh.

May 22, 2011
A powerful tornado hits Joplin, Missouri, causing billions of dollars in damages.

2000

May 31, 2013
The largest tornado in U.S. history touches down in El Reno, Oklahoma.

Test Your Knowledge

1 What are three massive storms that are similar to a tornado?

A. Cyclone, hurricane, or typhoon

2 How many tornadoes occur in the United States every year?

A. 1,000

3 What is a person called that chases tornadoes?

A. Tornado chaser

4 What is the area of the United States called where most tornadoes touch down?

A. Tornado Alley

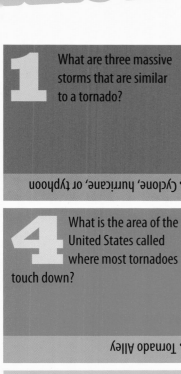

5 In what seasons do most tornadoes occur?

A. Spring or summer

6 What scale measures tornado damage?

A. Fujita Scale

7 Who created the Fujita Scale?

A. Dr. Tetsuya Theodore Fujita

8 In which direction do tornadoes in the northern hemisphere rotate?

A. Clockwise

9 What is the ring around the eye of the tornado called?

A. Annulus

10 What are some supplies you should put in your tornado disaster kit?

A. Bottled water, bandages, gauze, flashlight, batteries, scissors, and tissue

Create a Tornado Disaster Kit

When a tornado hits, you may not have much time to prepare. You won't have time to go out and buy supplies. Therefore it is important to keep a tornado disaster kit ready at all times. If you prepare in advance then you are ready for an emergency if a disaster strikes. Here are a few things to keep in mind.

1 Keep your tornado disaster kit in a sturdy box like a tool kit or tackle box. Prepare your disaster kit before an emergency strikes. Keep it stocked. Keep it in a dry safe place.

2 Put your disaster kit in a place where you can easily access it. The basement is a good place because that is probably where you will seek shelter.

3 Test your kit before you use it. Do a trial run of finding shelter and getting out the disaster kit. Make sure you have included the necessary items.

4 The main thing is to survive the tornado. Include things that will help in your goal of survival.

5 Do not use matches or a lighter since a tornado could cause a gas leak

What You Need
- Soap
- Bottled water
- Aspirin
- Band aids
- Sterile Gauze
- Splint
- First aid book
- Scissors
- Tissues
- Needle and thread
- Pocket knife
- Flashlight
- Extra batteries
- Radio
- Packaged food

Key Words

atmosphere: the layers of air and other gases that surrounds the Earth

closed circulation: counter clockwise winds blowing around a center

elders: people of older age often thought to be figures of authority within a group

epicenter: the center of the storm

frequency: the number of times something occurs

funnel cloud: clouds that rotate in a circular motion

hemisphere: half of a sphere; often refers to the upper and lower halves of Earth

meteorologists: scientists who study Earth's atmosphere and how weather systems work

pioneer: one of the first people to do something new

plains: areas of wide open and flat lands, made up mostly of grasses and very few trees

Index

Log on to www.av2books.com

AV² by Weigl brings you media enhanced books that support active learning. Go to www.av2books.com, and enter the special code found on page 2 of this book. You will gain access to enriched and enhanced content that supplements and complements this book. Content includes video, audio, weblinks, quizzes, a slide show, and activities.

AV² Online Navigation

Audio
Listen to sections the book read al[...]

Book Pages
AV² pages directly correspond to pages in the book.

Video
Watch informative video clips.

Key Words
Study vocabulary, and complete a matching word activity.

Embedded Weblinks
Gain additional information for research.

Try This!
Complete activities and hands-on experiments.

Quizzes
Test your knowledge.

Slide Show
View images and captions, and prepare a presentation.

AV² was built to bridge the gap between print and digital. We encourage you to tell us what you like and what you want to see in the future.

Sign up to be an AV² Ambassador at www.av2books.com/ambassador.